CREATING
S P A C E

for
Fast Business Success

32 Fast, Easy-to-Implement Tips to
Help You Make Time for
Work, Family & Fun!

WESTON LYON

Creating Space
for Fast Business Success

A Weston Lyon Book

Copyright © 2010, Weston Lyon Enterprises

All rights reserved.

Book Cover created and designed by
Tracey Miller *(www.TraceOfStyle.com)*

ISBN:145151574X
EAN-13: 9781451515749

Creating Space
for these special people...

To my son, Haven:
You're the best thing that's ever happened to me. It's always an awesome day when you're around. I love you with all my heart, munchkin!

To my friend and co-author, Diana:
Thank you for always being there...treating me like a son. And, thank you for being so gracious as I take our original masterpiece and apply it elsewhere!

Creating Space
Table of Contents

Read this First!

Have you ever said to yourself, "So much to do...and no time to get it all done?"

As an entrepreneur, I bet you have a lot of "to do's" in your life. You have so much to get done, but it feels like time just keeps on ticking.

I assure you time will not stop – though we all wish it did at times. We all have a finite amount of time every week. So how do some people get more done than others? How do some people seem to move through life with ease, while others struggle?

I'm not going to tell you I have all the answers...I wish we did, but I don't. What I can tell you is this:

Life is not about _doing_
Life is about _living!_

Now, each and every one of us has a different outlook on life. We all value life's delights in a different way. And, we all prioritize those delights in the order of importance that suits our life.

That's why I wrote this book. A while back, after a heart-break, I realized life is about living. I realized life is about what's important to us, individually. However, the problem most of us face is:

We don't have the time for what's important!?!

This book is the key to creating that time. This book is the key to creating the space you need in your life to do the things you really want to do.

Inside this book you'll find the tips, tricks, and strategies for making time – for what's important in YOUR life. Enjoy the journey and please let me know how this book affects your life.

Weston Lyon

How to Use This Book

This book serves as a quick resource of ideas to help you create space for what is truly important, each and every day.

As you read, highlight or underline the ideas that make sense in your life. Circle the actions that you feel would be manageable for you.

There are many different ideas and not all of them will work for everyone. At this point, you want to concentrate on what will work *for you*, right now.

WARNING! There are so many great ideas, that you will end up circling many that you could use.

When you finish reading, go back through and pick *three* of your favorite ideas and list them here:

1. _____
2. _____
3. _____

Now pick one action to begin with **right now.** This will be your first action and I urge you to give it at least one week to see how it works in your life.

If it works, keep doing it. If you have trouble with it, examine your attempt/action a little closer. Are you honestly giving it a chance? Are you putting up road-blocks or truly trying to create space?

After examining it, if you really think that this action will not work for you, go on to another idea.

Once you have incorporated one new action into your life and are seeing the results, you are ready to go on to your next action. Once you see the amazing results that come from creating space in your life, go back through this book and take on a few more ideas.

You may want to add a new action each week, or every two weeks, or once a month – it's up to you. You may even start thinking of your own ways to create more space in your life. If you do let me know...I'd love to hear from you!

By taking these actions, you will notice less stress and more happiness in your life. By creating space, you are opening yourself up to amazing and wonder-ful possibilities for a truly *Outstanding Life.*

Beyond this point are life changing, time making tips, tricks, and strategies...

Enter at your own risk!

Once you've read past this point, you have NO excuse not to live the life you deserve and desire.

Time Blocking

The sculpture is already inside the stone.

Michelangelo

Time blocking changed my life. I remember talking to a mentor of mine, David L. Holzer, about not being able to have the time to write my first book.

He asked me, *"Have you ever used time blocking?"*

"What is time blocking?" I questioned.

David said, *"Time blocking is when you sit down with your schedule and block out x amount of time to do a project of importance. For example, if you want to write your book faster, block out 3-4 hours once a week. That way you know when you're going to write."*

"That's genius!" I said.

You see, I had good intentions of writing my book in a timely manner. However, every time I wanted to write, something else got in the way.

With time blocking I was able to knock out my first book in less than 60 days. How do you start blocking your time? It's as easy as 1, 2, 3...

1. Choose an activity that is important to you

2. Take out your schedule and block out the amount of time you want to dedicate to this activity

3. Make a commitment to yourself to NEVER give this time to anyone or anything else

It's really that simple. Try it now with one activity of importance. Then use time blocking for the other activities that are important in your life. Here are some examples of what I use time blocking for:

- **Exercise**
- **Writing**
- **Meeting with clients**
- **Meeting with referral partners**
- **Meetings in general**
- **Playing with my son, Haven**
- **Relaxing**
- **Getting a massage**
- **Spending time with my family**
- **Martial arts practice**

The list goes on and on. I started with my writing time to finish my first book. Now, I time block everything!

What can you use time blocking for?
Brainstorm some ideas here:

_____

_____

_____

_____

Plan Your Day

It is the choices you make today
that are creating...your future.
Shad Helmstetter

Not only do you want to start blocking your time...
you also want to start planning your time.

Every night before you go to bed look at your schedule
for the next day. Take the following steps to plan
your next day for success:

1. Write down 5 things you feel are important to get
done

2. Prioritize them in the order they need to get done
(1 being the most important and 5 being the least
important)

3. Block time for your first 3 items

When you wake up, make sure you review this list
one more time, so you know what you're doing.
Then:

1. Take action on your #1 priority until it's DONE!

2. Then, and only then, move to priority numero dos.

3. Then, and only then, move to priority numero tres.

If you get done with your first 3 priorities, **congratulations!!!**

Most people never accomplish that much important stuff in one day. Now, move onto priorities four and five.

Do this every day and watch how much more you get done. I guarantee you'll succeed faster, get noticed more, and feel better than you ever thought possible.

Procrastination is a Killer

Success is waiting for you

to make the first move.

John Maxwell

Okay, I admit it...I love to procrastinate. It's human nature to do so. However, procrastinating will kill your chances at succeeding in life.

This is what happens when you procrastinate: **First**, you delay your success. For example, if you put off writing down what's important in your life you'll delay your success in achieving it.

It doesn't mean you won't have success. It means you'll have to wait longer to get it.

Second, you set yourself up to feel rushed and then stressed. For example, if you put off getting gas in your car, you'll feel stressed out when you have to be somewhere and need to get gas (before you have to walk). I've been in this situation before. It sucks.

Third, you condition yourself to keep putting things off. This is probably the worst of the three.

When you procrastinate, and eventually get the job done later; you condition yourself to keep procrastinating because you know you can get the job done again.

This conditioning creates a never-ending cycle. If you get caught in the cycle, life will not be very fun. So, how do you get over procrastination?

You decide to take action now!

That's it. It's simple, but it's the truth. I made this decision a few years ago, and it's been one of the best decisions of my life.

It's your turn. Make the decision to take action on whatever you have at hand. Do it. Get it done. Succeed. And break the habit of procrastination once and for all.

(Note: You don't want to take action on every "to do" item in your life. Just the important tasks. Let's cover that next...)

Important, NOT Urgent

Either you run the day
or the day runs you.
J.C. McPheeters

If you want to take stress out of your life and make life more fulfilling, you MUST learn the difference between things being important and urgent, and how to harmonize them.

No offense to Webster, but here are my definitions in terms of actions to be taken:
Important – actions that get you closer to your desired result
Urgent – actions that need to be done immediately

Okay, let's first take a look at the difference between them. Important actions get you closer to your desired result. Isn't that what life is all about – achieving results you want to happen.

On the other hand, urgent actions need to be done immediately. Some important actions are urgent too; however, most urgent actions won't get you any closer to your desired result. In fact, most actions that are urgent take you away from your desired result and closer to someone else's desired result.

So how do we harmonize them?
First, you need to know what you want.
Second, you need to be committed to what you want.
Finally, you need to be flexible.

Like I said before, life happens. It's unfortunate, but people die, hearts get broken, and so on. Here's a common sense example of how to harmonize:

You're getting ready to go exercise (because it's really important) and you get a phone call from your best friend.

His/her significant other just broke his/her heart. What do you do? Go work out and call your friend later or get your butt over to comfort them? You go work out...*just kidding!*

Of course you go comfort your friend. It's not important (by the definition above), but it is certainly urgent.

Go to your friend now and work out later. Listen, your friend needs you now – urgent. Your body needs exercise sometime that day – important. Just work out later and you'll be good to go.

That's being flexible. That's being in harmony with life's little nuances. You're acting on the urgent stuff in crisis, but NOT just for the hell of it.

Tend to urgent matters when needed, but <u>take action on important items 90-95% of the time</u> and you'll be well on your way.

Learn to be Lazy

I make no secret of the fact that
I would rather lie on a sofa than sweep
beneath it. But you have to be efficient
if you're going to be lazy.
Shirley Conran

We talked about important vs. urgent. Now, let's look at important vs. unimportant.

If important actions get you closer to your desired result, then unimportant actions get you nowhere near your desired result.

So my solution is:

Learn to be lazy!

I don't mean be a bum. I mean learn to be lazy about activities that don't really matter in life (in the big picture). Actions that don't get you what you really want. This is where you can procrastinate. Here's a list of the tasks that are unimportant in my life:

- **Washing dishes**
- **Cutting grass**
- **Washing my car**
- **Cleaning my house**
- **Organizing my desk**
- **And much, much more**

I hate doing these activities. They are NOT getting me any closer to the results I want.

Therefore, I don't do them...or I'm lazy at doing them. I wait until the last possible minute to do some of them, and others I give to someone else to do.

It's not because I can't. It's because I'd rather spend my time here on this planet taking action on the things I want to do!

Learning to be lazy will help you create space in your life for your desired results. What are some things you could learn to be lazy about? List them here:

_____

_____

_____

_____

_____

_____

_____

_____

_____

_____

_____

_____

_____

_____

_____

Demand It!

The secret to getting absolutely anything
you want is simple: do whatever it takes.

Mike Hernacki

State your demands, **first to yourself** and then to others. Make creating space for an outstanding life a priority.

You have to totally embrace the idea that YOU are important and that YOUR time, YOUR desires, and YOUR needs are important.

Until you insist on this, nothing will change.

People are very busy with their own lives. The people you live with, your co-workers and your friends are all busy.

Even the people closest to you are not going to be thinking of your needs every day. It is up to you to make your wishes known and stick to your guns.

Tell yourself that you will have time every single day. It does not matter if you believe this right away.

Once you start changing your thoughts, your brain will start making the thoughts come true.

You will discover opportunities and come up with all sorts of ideas to help you find time.

People may not understand it, but they will begin to respect it. They may not like it, but everyone will benefit from it.

YOU are important. You are worth it. Demand it!

List some things that are important in your life that you haven't demanded:

_____

_____

_____

_____

_____

_____

_____

_____

_____

_____

_____

_____

_____

_____

_____

Now, let them be known.

Step Away from the Phone

Often short term gain

produces long term pain.

Anonymous

We've all been conditioned to answer the phone as soon as we hear it ring.

My son, who's only 7 years old, is already conditioned to do this. Why? Because he sees the grown-ups around him race for the phone as soon as they hear it like a dog chasing a fake rabbit at the track.

We have a big family so my son gets to experience a lot of different environments. When he's with me, I try to break him of this habit. Why?

Because having the habit of always answering the phone when it rings creates problems in your life. Here are a few problems to keep in mind:

Answering the phone can interrupt your thoughts - If you're brainstorming or daydreaming, don't answer the phone! Your thoughts are way more important than whoever is on the end of the line. If you're meditating, turn the phone off. Silence is golden.

Answering the phone takes time away from important tasks - If you're in the middle of something important, don't answer the phone! An important task takes precedence over any phone call.

Answering the phone can drain your energy -
This may sound silly, but the person on the other end
may drain your energy. Maybe it's a telemarketer
who makes you angry. Maybe it's a family member
asking for money (like that's never happened to you).
Whatever the case may be, don't let this happen to
you.

Final thoughts: Step away from the phone and
enjoy what you're doing in the moment. If you are
expecting an important call, at least have Caller ID to
make sure it's the right person.

Everyone can leave a message. It's no big deal. They
would do it anyway if you weren't available.

Once and For All, Set Up Your Work Areas

Short as life is, we make it still shorter by the careless waste of time.

Victor Hugo

How much time do you spend looking for what you need every time you start a project or task? What a waste of time!

You go to do some cleaning, and you left your supplies in another room. You are ready to start a job fixing something, and you cannot find the tools you need to start, let alone finish. You go into your office and nothing is where you thought you left it.

At this point, you look at the clock and realize that by the time you assemble everything you need, you will be late, rushed, or unable to finish, yet again.

It's time to get organized.

Break the organizing into small steps and do it once and for all. Think of the trouble spots. Where do you get slowed down the most? Housework, household repairs, paperwork?

Start with the one that bothers you the most, and go to that area. Make a list of all the supplies you need.

If the supplies are in the house, assemble them. Assembling may take time, but keep at it until you are done. Make a plan to go to the store and get everything else to fill in the gaps. While you are there, buy containers and boxes to hold the supplies.

Keep your supplies for specific projects in the same place, at all times. You can even put a warning, like **DO NOT TOUCH**, on them if you anticipate problems...I swear my mom has OCD, so if she visits, this is a must – she's worse than my son at moving stuff around.

If you are overwhelmed, there are professional organizers who do this work. They are able to help you "zero in" on the trouble spots and give you good, solid suggestions on how to become more organized.

NOTE: If you live in Pittsburgh and you're interested in hiring someone like this, let me know and I'll tell you who to contact.

Once you have your tools in place for all projects, you will save huge amounts of time. Now, go organize what needs done, so you can save time in the future.

Get off the Computer

If you're spending more time looking
at a screen than in the eyes of another
human being...STOP IT!
Weston Lyon

I'm guilty myself at times, but we have to learn to get off the computer. We use the computer at home. We use the computer at work. Heck, I've even used my laptop in the bathroom when I was swamped and needed a quiet space (embarrassing, but true).

Here's what to do so you can create more space in your life...without the computer.

1. Buy a digital timer. (They're cheap.)

2. Put it beside you when you're on the computer and make sure you activate it.

3. Notice and write down how much time you spend with this inanimate object, your computer.

I guarantee that it will surprise you at first. What surprised me the most was how much time I was spending checking e-mail. (We'll get to this in a moment.)

Now that you know how much time you're spending in front of the computer do this:

Make a list of activities that take the same amount of time. For example, if you spend 2 hours in front a computer every day, what activity can you do in that same amount of time?

- Can you go exercise instead?
- Can you continue reading your favorite novel?

- Can you spend time with your wife, husband, or significant other?
- Can you enjoy time with your kids?

What can YOU do with that time? Make a list:

_____

_____

_____

_____

_____

_____

_____

_____

_____

_____

_____

_____

_____

You probably won't be able to get away from your computer for the entire amount of time, but you will be able to cut back and enjoy life more now that you know this.

Now, let's conquer e-mail...

E-mail and S&R Disorder

All our lauded technological progress –
our very civilization – is like the axe in
the hand of the pathological criminal.
Albert Einstein

I'm convinced e-mail is evil.

It's the biggest time waster we have today. In fact, it's even responsible for a new disorder that has developed over the past 10 years...

It's called **S&R Disorder**. Or more common called Send &
Receive Disorder (thank you Ali Brown for alerting me to this disorder).

Here's how to diagnose it:
• If you have e-mail alerts every time an e-mail is sent to you...
you have S&R Disorder

• If you check your e-mail first thing in the morning...
you have S&R Disorder

• If you check your e-mails every time you walk in the room...
you have S&R Disorder

This disorder is unfortunately common today. Hundreds of millions of people from around the globe have already been affected by this disorder.

Don't be another statistic! Take action. Here's how to save yourself from "e-mail the evil":

1. Disable the feature that allows e-mail to flow into your computer without your knowledge; as well as the "alert" to new e-mail dinger (annoying!)

2. Stop checking e-mail in the morning and start checking e-mail later in the day; preferably after lunch. Leave the morning open for important tasks.

3. Check and respond to e-mail everyday that's important to you and your business. However, only respond to the unimportant email when it's convenient for you...this is a good item to time block.

Will this be easy? Of course not!

But if you want to create space for more important things in your life and live stress-free, you have to learn to control email!

Once under control, you'll find NOT checking email as often to be exhilarating and freeing.

Do Not Read Every E-mail

Any idiot can send an e-mail...

I should know I send plenty.

BUT, that doesn't mean

you should read them all.

Weston Lyon

We talked about e-mail before being evil.
Here's another lesson about e-mail:

Do not read every one!

I'm sure you get tons of e-mail. I get hundreds a day.
And I used to spend all my time reading them. Wow,
what a waste of time!

Certain e-mails are probably necessary (depending on
what you do for a living). Others waste your valuable
time.

Eliminate these from your inbox and create tons of
time in your life. Don't read them...just delete them!

How do you know which ones to delete? While I bet
you can already guess, here's a crash course in
deleting email:

Delete the spam. Emails that come from people you
don't know (or subject lines that don't make sense);
emails that come from suspicious addresses; and
emails that are spelled in ALL CAPS.

Delete the ones that raise your blood pressure.
You know what I'm talking about...there's always 1-2
people who send you annoying emails. Delete them
and rid yourself of the unwanted stress.

Delete the ones that have that stupid FW: in front of them. Again, you know what I'm talking about...you probably receive your fair share of these on a regular basis. Some may be funny, but the majority are not. They're time vampires. Put a stake through them before you get bit.

IMPORTANT NOTE: If you send tons of e-mail, like me, make sure they ADD VALUE to people.

If they don't, then people will delete them without reading them...as well they should!

Put that thing away

If you keep doing that…you'll go blind!

Anonymous

In addition to email and computers, we now have to deal with smart phones.

Put that thing away!

Do you really need to read emails and texts every moment of the day? This is unhealthy. Seriously!

Here are some reasons you may want to consider putting that damn crackberry away:

1. You're shortening your attention span. If you're constantly being interrupted by your phone (calls, texts, pings, etc.), you'll eventually create the bad habit of always playing with your phone.

2. You're frying your brain. Your brain is meant to function at extremely high levels; however, it's also meant to have breaks for rest. Always having your brain "on" is bad for you. Give it time to rest. Give it time to think. Give it time to do nothing.

3. You're losing your creative ability. When your brain is constantly on the go between talking, texting, and whatever else you're doing, you don't have time to think. And, when that happens, you lose your creative juices. You lose the practice of thinking creatively.

4. You're one step away from evolving into the next human being...homo sapien to homo thumbs. Yes, that's right. A human being with BIG thumbs!

Seriously, put that thing away. Give your thumbs a rest. Give your brain a rest.

Use this 'down time' to do something else you enjoy. Maybe you can finish this book (haha). Maybe you can sit in the dark by yourself and embrace the silence. Maybe you can drop and give yourself 20!

Trust me. There are more important things to do before you die than check your email, text your address book, or surf the web.

Plan Your Errands

Everything is created twice –
first mentally, then physically.

Greg Anderson

Here is another simple, yet effective action that not enough people use. **Plan ahead with errands and necessary stops.**

Over the weekend, before your week begins, think about tasks that have to be done outside the home during the upcoming week.

If they are chores that you cannot delegate, plan how they will be accomplished. Make a list of all the out-of-the-home tasks.

If you are dropping clothing at the cleaners, assemble them and put them in your vehicle. If you are returning movies or library books, put them in bags, label them, and put them in your vehicle.

Returns to a store? Attach the receipt carefully to the bag with a stapler or tape, and, yes, again put them in your vehicle.

Now take your list, and think about your plans for the week. When will you be in the area where the errands have to be done? How can you combine them with work schedules, children's schedules, etc?

Make use of all the times you will be driving right by the cleaners, library, recycling depository, and plan ahead.

This simple ten minute organization can save you time in the morning as you are trying to get out the door to work.

It will save you time, driving back home for all the items you forgot. It will create space in your day to do fun things like read or relax.

Make a list of the places you go on a regular basis. Beside each place, write down what you typically need when you get there:

_____

_____

_____

_____

_____

_____

_____

_____

_____

_____

_____

Having these details will save you time. In addition, if you need assistance at some point (broken arm, pregnant, or just no more time left), you can hand these details to someone else and THEY CAN GO FOR YOU.

It's OK to Say No

No means yes, seriously.

Anonymous

Why do we have so much trouble saying no? And how much trouble do we get into when we can't say no?

Learning to say no can bring us to a great place in our lives. We create more space and more time, which can lead to more energy and happier lives.

We are fearful of saying no for many reasons:
- **We don't want to hurt someone's feelings.**
- **We want to feel needed.**
- **We really want to do it.**
- **We feel bad actually saying it.**
- **We don't want to miss out on something.**
- **We don't want to disappoint.**

But learning to say no more often and at the right times, will enable us to create more time for what is really important in our lives.

By saying no to some things, you are saying YES to some very important things.

Yes to more time for ourselves. Yes to more time for our health. Yes to more time for what we decide is truly important.

Saying no takes practice. A good way to begin is to say it once a day to one request.

Later, you can expand this exercise and start saying no to yourself:
No, I know I will feel bad if I eat that food.
No, I know I need my rest more than I need to watch that movie.
No, soda is not good for me. I will have water instead.

No can be delayed while you get up your courage...

Wait fifteen minutes to give an answer to a request or invitation. Wait one day, if you need that time to practice.

Some of us are so used to saying yes and being agree-able; we have forgotten how to say no. Practice.

Remember, saying no sometimes is saying YES to all sorts of possibilities!

Everything in Its Place

I'd lose my head if it weren't attached.

Anonymous

An easy way to create space in your day is to stop wasting time looking for objects.

How much time do you waste looking for the same items, every day, over and over? Keys, cell phone, Blackberry, etc.

Decide on a place for these items and always keep them there. Sounds simple, but so many of us do not follow this rule, and we spend way too much time looking for lost items and getting frantic on our way out the door.

Right now, make a list of some of the items you need to have a place for (keys, schedule, paperwork). Beside each item, jot down where you plan on making space for these:

_____

_____

_____

_____

_____

_____

_____

_____

_____

_____

_____

In addition to your items, children and students could find one spot for their backpacks and school supplies.

Every night, backpacks, lunches and projects can be put in the same place, preferably near the door, so there is no last minute freaking out before the day even begins.

Starting the day in a calm fashion can set the tone for a great day. Feeling organized and together as you leave your home to face the world is a fantastic way to begin your latest adventure in living an outstanding life.

Feels good, doesn't it?

Exercise at Home

Time is your most valuable asset.

Don't waste a single moment.

Weston Lyon

Exercising at home will give you, literally, months of your life back.

First, exercising is a MUST if you want to create an outstanding life. Without your health, nothing else really matters.

Second, exercising at home saves you hours a week which add up quickly. Let's take a look at this simple, yet astonishing calculation:

Let's say you exercise at your local gym and the gym is 10 minutes away from you. That means you're in route to the gym and from the gym for 20 minutes total.

If you work out only 3 times a week you waste 1 hour of your life every week on drive time.

That's 52 hours a year. And 520 hours every ten years. That means in a ten-year period you waste over 21 FULL days driving to the gym and back to work out.

Imagine if you just exercised at home? You'd create 52 hours a year of new space. And over 21 FULL days of new space in a ten year period.

What could you do with that amount of time? Oy vey!

There are tons of books and courses on exercising at home, including my own course, <u>The Fastest Workout Ever</u>.

Get mine or someone else's material and get to work. You'll love the results you get in terms of your health; as well as how much time you'll save!

****

To get you started, here are some exercises to try at home (of course, see your doctor before engaging in any activity!):

Walking in Place
Pushups
Sit-ups
Chair Dips
Shadow Boxing
Dancing
Deep Breathing

Exercise with Your Children

A little nonsense now and then
is relished by the wisest men.
Willy Wonka

I can go on and on about the benefits of exercise for you and your child; however let's not focus on that right now. Instead, let's take a look at how exercising with your child will create space in your life.

Exercising with your child allows you to accomplish two important goals at one time. One, you're able to spend quality time with your child; and two, you're able to get your exercise in for the day while having a great time.

Here are 3 things I love doing with my son that you can take and do, or adapt, for your child:

Dancing – My son loves to dance. Unlike his dad, he has fantastic rhythm.

If you've ever danced before, you know its great exercise. And when you add in swinging your child, dipping your child, and lifting your child as you dance you have one terrific, awesome, outstanding exercise session that kicks your butt!

Playing at the Park – This is one of our favorite activities to do. In fact, when it's spring and summer and you can't find us...we're at the park.

Playing at the park isn't just for kids of small stature. It's also for big kids, like me!

You can run, jump, and swing. You can play freeze tag (our favorite), hide and go seek, or whatever your imagination creates.

Have fun. Be a kid. Live!

Using Bodyweight Exercises – These are my specialty (I've written several books on the subject), so we do a lot of these wherever we go.

Exercises like Pushups, Squats, Lunges, and a slew of other exercises ranging from easy to extremely hard.

Your children will fall in love with these activities when they see how much fun you're both having.

And, as an extra bonus, you can make the exercises harder by using your child. For example, I lift Haven overhead while doing squats –killer workout!

As you can see, we do a lot of exercise in my house. And we have a lot of FUN! Go for it, and write to me with your creative adventures.

Note: If you don't have kids pass this on to a parent you know…they'll love you for it.

Get Help!

I not only use all the brains that I have,
but all that I can borrow.

Woodrow Wilson

Getting help can come in many forms. Let's take a look at two ways to get help so you can create more space in your life:

Personal Assistants

Personal Assistants can do whatever you need to have done. They can wash clothes. They can cook food. They can take care of the kids when you need a break. They can even go grocery shopping for you!

A Personal Assistant may be right for you. Think of some things you hate doing and could hire a PA for:

_____

_____

_____

_____

_____

_____

Virtual Assistants

Like Personal Assistants, Virtual Assistants can help you get the mundane tasks done that you don't like to do.

The difference is VA's are invisible. Sort of. VA's are assistants that work out of their own home and you never (or rarely) see them.

They're great if you have tasks that can be done without being present. For example, I use a virtual assistant to post announcements and such on my websites. I can do it, but why waste my time when I can get someone else to do it?

Another thing you can use VA's for is research. Let's say you wanted to research some healthy recipes for your family but didn't have the time. Hire a VA to research for you.

See how easy it is to create time? And it's fun too once you get the hang of it.

IMPORTANT NOTE: Hiring a personal or virtual assistant is not only good to help you create space, it's an excellent way to directly affect the economy.

Hiring someone stimulates growth in the economy. You're putting money in the system to be passed around. And, you're creating a win-win situation.

You get the work done you don't want to take the time to complete and the assistant gets to do something they love - what a concept!

Ask for Help!

If I had to do it all over again –

I'd get help!

Anonymous

I used to be too proud to ask other people for help.
I thought I could do it all. Wow, talk about stressing
myself out!

There are too many things to do in this world. And if
you don't know which things are more important to
you, you're screwed. You'll be stressed out and that's
not good.

Luckily, a few years ago I changed my ways. I was
listening to Jack Canfield's and Mark Victor Hansen's
audio series, The Aladdin Factor, and heard them
talking about asking for help.

They said, *"You have to A-S-K to G-E-T."*

Yes, they spelled that out. But that made it stick.
Hmmm...

You have to A-S-K to G-E-T

You have to "ask to get." If you DO NOT ask for help,
then you'll continue to be stressed. If you DO ask for
help, then you may get the help you need.

I know, I know. What if the person you ask says NO?
Who cares? You'll never know their answer until you
ask.

Get used to asking for help. The worst that can happen is you get rejected. No biggie.

Ask someone else. Your time is valuable. You have stuff you want. Create some time in your life by asking for help.

Make a list of some things that you need help doing. Beside each item, jot down who you know who may be able to help:

_____

_____

_____

_____

_____

_____

_____

_____

_____

_____

_____

_____

_____

Leverage OPT

To be effective, you must know
how to communicate your vision and
how to enlist the cooperation of others.
M.Z. Hackman

OPT = Other People's Time

You only have so much time in your day. Why not leverage other people's time to your advantage?

Here's what you do:
1. Make a list of things you have to do

2. Put a star next to the items YOU have to do

3. Put an "X" next to the items other people can do for you

4. Delegate these items to people you work with or family members

Your time is precious. And it should be used to accomplish the tasks that you are the best at; activities that make you money; or activities that please you.

Everything else can be delegated! Everything else can be leveraged using OPT.

Try it. I bet you'll like it.

Delegation Calculator

YOU + OPT = MORE TIME AND LESS STRESS

Enjoy Customer Service

You only get what you give yourself –

so give yourself the best.

Dr Robert Anthony

Do you know there are businesses out there that want to serve you? It's true. I learned this a few years ago from a friend of mine who hates to grocery shop.

We were talking one day when she mentioned, *"I hate to shop!"*

"You hate to shop?" I asked

"Well, I love shopping for clothes, but I hate shopping for food," she replied. *"That's why I have Sam's Club do all my shopping for me."*

"What do you mean?" I inquired.

She went on to tell me that Sam's Club does her shopping and all she has to do is pick it up and pay the bill. She simply calls their pick-up hotline, gives them her list, and picks it up soon thereafter.

What a service!

And Sam's Club isn't the only business out there that wants to serve you. A friend of mine in Maryland uses a Dry Cleaner that has pick-up and drop-off services. Talk about saving time!

Check your area for businesses like these that want
to serve you. I bet you'll be pleasantly surprised
when you start looking.

Again, your time is precious. Don't waste it on
errands and chores that other people can do – in this
case, WANT to do.

They want your business. Give it to them, so you can
live the life you want to live.

Children and How to Use Them

What do we live for, if it is not to
make life less difficult for each other?

George Eliot

Written by my friend, Diana Fletcher:

We love them. They are treasures. We would do anything for them. But let's face it. They add to the
work load. So let's see how we can turn things
around and let our children help us.

A good investment with your time, and to create more
space for healthier living, is to teach children to do
chores and take responsibility for some housework.
This time investment will pay off in dividends.

Children can start when they are small and eager to
please. This eagerness to please does not always
continue into the teen-age years - teach them when
they are young!

Here are some ideas to get you started. (You will
think of more, I am sure, once you get the hang of it.):

**Little ones can help fold towels and carry
things.** They can be taught to put away their toys
and make their beds. They can learn to set the table
and help clear it.

Children can be taught to make simple meals.
Breakfast is the easiest with cereal and fruit, and
they can work their way up to safely using the
toaster.

Lunch can be simple sandwiches and later you can teach them simple dinners. Do not expect perfection

Older children, who can drive, can do errands and grocery shopping. Even those who cannot drive can help with errands. I have hired my fourteen year old daughter to do the grocery shopping and to put away the groceries. All she needs is the ride to and from the grocery store. I gain a couple hours, and she earns money and learns valuable life skills. Win,win!

Many times, as parents, we have the idea that no one can do our job as well as we can, around the house, in the kitchen, and everywhere else. While that fact may be true, who cares?

If you are driving yourself nuts and getting stressed about doing everything perfectly, you are the one who suffers. Lighten up, get help, and use the time you gain to make yourself happier. Everyone in your life will benefit.

Stop Accepting Every Invitation

When you feel driven to act on
an impulse, take your time to ask if this
is really what is in your best interest.
Eknath Easwaran

Do you really have to accept every invitation that comes your way? Do you really have to go to every networking event you hear about? Is it really that important to be everywhere that other people want you to be?

There are different reasons for attending events or parties. Some of them are valid.

Perhaps it is a networking event, and you truly see some advantages for your business. Perhaps the people that are going to be at a party are people you absolutely love and enjoy being with. Perhaps it is a family gathering and it is truly important to others that you show up.

But sometimes, and more often than we like to admit, we really do not have to attend an event and we do anyway.

Take some time to think. When you receive an invitation or notice of an upcoming event, stop and think:

- **Will I regret going/not going?**

- **Will I be too tired the next day to fully participate in my life?**

- **Will it be worth it in terms of work, relation-ships, and happiness?**

- **Do I truly want to invest my time in this ac-tivity?**

After thinking about these questions, if you want to go, by all means, go! But if you feel you have to do it, analyze those reasons.

Will it really hurt someone's feelings, or will she/he care that much? Will there be another opportunity to take part in this activity or is this the only time you can do this?

As far as business, is it important for you to be there? Many times, we are on automatic and agree to participate in activities that do not help us live out-standing lives.

We end up with less sleep, we may overindulge in food or drink, and we may take time away from the people in our lives who are truly important.

Just take the time to think. Remember, **how you spend the minutes of your life, is how you spend your life.**

Keep Healthy Food Handy

When we don't take a few minutes,
and that is all it takes, to plan ahead,
all we can do is react in ways that don't
lend themselves to healthy living.

Diana Fletcher

If you learn to keep food handy, you'll save a ton of time - not to mention a ton of money. Here are a few ideas to help you keep food handy:

Keep food in your car
You can keep meal replacement bars, a can of nuts, water, and other healthy snacks handy in your car if you plan ahead.

You won't get hungry and feel the urge to stop by your local fast food joint. Think about the time it will save you too.

Keep food at work
You can keep even more food at work. You can keep oatmeal, raisins, nuts, seeds, natural peanut butter, lean meats (if you have a refrigerator), fruits, and much more.

By doing so, you'll be able to eat healthier, while creating time for yourself. Think about it. How much time do you waste at the vending machine or driving to lunch? Use this extra time for yourself – enjoy it.

Pack your lunch
I carry a cooler with me every day I'm on the road. I bring meal replacement bars, fruit, nuts and raisins, and much more with me.

Doing this keeps me on my eating schedule, while saving me time, money and energy. I don't have to look for a place to eat...I have it with me!

Also, I bring a cooler when I take the kids (my son and his friends) to the park in the summer. Why feed them fast food when we can pack a healthy lunch. **Picnic time, anyone!?**

Make a list of what healthy foods you can keep handy at these specific places:

In the Car:

_____

_____

_____

_____

At Work:

_____

_____

_____

_____

In a cooler:

_____

_____

_____

_____

Write It Down!

Spinning more plates doesn't increase
your talent – it only increases your
likelihood of dropping a plate.

Anonymous

How much time do we waste trying to remember things? This time waster could be the biggest space stealer of all.

Trying to remember what we needed at the store, trying to remember what was said at the meeting, trying to remember what someone asked you to bring to the party...not only do we waste time trying to remember, but we then waste time retracing our steps to find the stuff we forgot to bring, and it goes on and on.

Very simple idea: Carry a notebook and...

Write everything down

This doesn't have to be complicated or annoying.

- **You jot down the times and dates from the meeting.**

- **You jot down grocery items as you think of them.**

- **You jot down errands that you want to do.**

- **You jot down the woman's name you keep forgetting.**

You carry a notebook with you and keep track of your life. Notebooks come in all sizes, from pocket-size to briefcase size. I suggest smaller, but you have to find what works for you.

Stop wasting time trying to catch up with what you forgot. Let a notebook create some extra space in your day. Use that time for living a better, more outstanding life!

Stop Perfecting

The goal of a winner should
be excellence – not perfection.

Dr. Robert Anthony

I'm not perfect. You're not perfect. And nothing else is ever perfect!

Stop trying to perfect life; it's a waste of time. You'll never achieve perfection and trying to will only drive you buggy. Here's a phrase to always keep with you:

Good enough...is good enough

I learned this from Dan Kennedy. When I first heard this, I was a bit stunned. In fact, I didn't really internalize it for several weeks. Then it hit me. He wasn't saying "don't try your best." He was saying "perfection is not possible, get things done and move on."

Wow! That may sound simple, but that's powerful stuff. Here's an example that illustrates getting something done and moving on:

When I wrote my first book, I did some editing. Then I sent it to a friend to edit it some more. When I got it back, I sent it in to get printed. And guess what happened?

The printer said, *"Do you know you have some misspellings?"*

I said, *"I had it edited twice. Just print the thing!"*

So why did I tell you this? Because perfection is
impossible. If it wasn't the spelling in the book, it
may have been the grammar. If it wasn't that, it
could have been something else. Who cares?

The information in that book (and every book I write
for that matter) is way more important than the
occasional misspellings and grammatical errors.

Again, I'm not saying I don't try (or that you
shouldn't). You should. You just need to be careful
shooting for perfection. Shot for excellence, not
perfection.

Get things done and everything will work out just
fine. Remember, good enough is good enough.

Here are several things that I don't worry about at
all. I just get 'em done without looking at every last
detail (or have someone else get them done):
- **Washing dishes**
- **Cutting grass**
- **Washing my car**
- **Cleaning my house**
- **Organizing my desk**
- **An much much more**

Note: I listed these same items when I talked about
learning to be lazy. Coincidence? I think not.

Quick Decisions

The truth is that there is never a really "right time"....there comes a time when one simply hopes for the best, pinches one's nose, and jumps into the abyss. If this were not so, we would not have needed to create the words heroine, hero, or courage.

Clarissa Pinkola Estes

If you want to create an outstanding life you have to learn to make quick decisions.

Will you always be right? No. But that's life. And the cool thing about being wrong is you learn from the experience.

In fact, I've learned way more from my mistakes than I've ever learned from my successes.

Decisions are a part of life. And, luckily, they're like building a muscle. The more decisions you make, the stronger your decision-making-muscle gets.

Go make a bunch of decisions today, and see where they take you. Do them quickly as an experiment and find out how good you are.

Over time you'll get better and you'll be having a blast with your quick decisions.

Note: Some decisions do take time to think about, so don't use this advice the wrong way. However, most of your decisions should be made quickly. There are not too many you can't fix if you make a mistake – so go wild and live!

Stop Talking

Listen to Life, and you will
hear the voice of life crying, Be!
James Dillet Freeman

How much time do we waste with unproductive talk?

I am not talking about time with good friends, sharing ideas and parts of our lives that truly interest us. I am talking about useless talk.

Useless talk includes gossiping and obsessive talk. Going over and over the same old, same old.

Talking about others in a negative way sends out bad energy and never really makes us feel good. Obsessing about the same problems with no eye on the solution is such a time waster.

Sometimes, we talk just to talk, and it helps no one. Going over and over bad stuff only makes us feel worse. Even going over and over good things can tire us out and the people who are forced to listen.

Quiet down and listen.

Creating space by quieting our voices can lead to truly rewarding results. **You may hear something amazing!**

TV: The Sneaky Time Stealer

No man's knowledge can
go beyond his experiences.
John Locke

Overall, we watch too much TV. We need to take back the time TV viewing is stealing from our lives.

As much as I say I don't like television, I do have some favorite shows and I do watch movies. I have learned various tricks to shorten the time TV takes from my daily life.

Enjoy the wonderful benefits of TiVo, DVR, and recording. You don't really have to watch a show when it is broadcast. Taping it and watching it later can give you back 15 to 20 minutes when you zap the commercials.

Recordings can be watched later when you are on the treadmill or exercise bike. You don't have to give up your shows and movies completely! I record <u>The Ellen Show</u> every day and watch it a day or so behind, when I eat my lunch or snacks throughout the day... 15-20 minute breaks for food and stretching...and laugh'n with Ellen!

Examine what you are really doing when you sit down to watch TV. Is this television viewing really a good way to spend your time? Is it really necessary to have it on every night? Are those programs really that good that you want to sit there staring in a state of hypnosis?

Pick some shows at the beginning of the week that will really be fun to see and only watch those. *Teach your children to do the same.*

People feel that they have to check the news programs every night. No, you don't.

As Gavin de Becker points out in his book <u>Fear Less</u>, the news business is a business. That business seems to be to scare us with fear-promoting TV news. The sensationalized headlines, the threat of terrorism, the pull to come back for more - you might miss something going on!

De Becker points out that if we turn it off, you may find you "are feeling happier, more courageous, more connected to the people you've chosen to have in your life."

He also points out, "If we turn it off, then we can face the important question, which is not how we might die, but rather, how shall we live? And that is up to us."

Limit your TV time for one week. See if you can have a couple nights with no TV at all. You may be very surprised with the results. Notice how much time you suddenly seem to have.

Overestimate Your Time

In life there are no over-achievers,
only under-estimators.

Anonymous

Overestimating time is a lesson I learned from my dad. Like most lessons I learned from him, it took a long time to sink in.

You know what I mean...being young you know everything there is to know, right? Ha ha! Actually, the older I get, the more I realize how little I know.

Anywho, you can create more space in your life if you overestimate the time you think you need to finish a project. There are two reasons for this:

1. Projects will always take longer than you think they will.

2. If you overestimate the time, you will not get time-crunched and ruin other plans you may have made for the day.

If you miraculously finish early, you have time to spare. This time to spare can open up other doors.

You can finish other important projects, or you can just relax and enjoy the extra time (wow, what a concept!)

Weston's Rule of Thumb

(actually Erwin Lyon's rule of thumb):

Give yourself 25% more time to finish a project

****

This may seem like you're filling space instead of creating space; but once you allow for this extra, you'll be pleasantly surprised how smoothly your projects get finished - and how little stress you feel..

Welcome the Spaces that are Being Created for You

It is only when we silence the blaring
sounds of our existence that we can
finally hear the whispers of truth that life
reveals to us, as it stands knocking
on the doorsteps of our hearts.

K.T. Jong

Learn to recognize the spaces that come naturally in your day. Long drives in the car, waiting in line for coffee, getting to a meeting early...these are all opportunities.

These spaces, or time chunks, are unexpected gifts and instead of getting impatient or mad, we should recognize them as the treasures they are. We have been given extra time!

We can read while waiting in a line; listen to books on CD in the car; jot down notes for projects while we wait for our dinner date.

We can just sit and think. We all need time to slow down. Use these built-in opportunities.

In fact, here's an opportunity right now before you finish this book...

Awww...

Feels good, huh?

How are You Spending You Days?

Efficiency is doing things right.

Effectiveness is doing the right things.

Alan Nelson

We have been in a hurry-up mode for so long that it is difficult for many of us to figure out how to slow down.

One great way to begin is to look at how you spend your days. Honestly look at how you spend each minute of every day. Often we have developed habits that no longer have any purpose.

Look at your activities and ask yourself, does this activity benefit me anymore? Does it benefit anyone else?

If you are honest with yourself, you will discover many of our activities are unnecessary or could be done by someone else.

Eliminating just a few of these unnecessary activities can create extra space in your day.

The purpose of this is not to immediately fill those moments with more work. The purpose is to create space to take care of your health, family, and other important priorities.

Once you have eliminated time wasters, you can create a life of good health, happiness, and joy.

Remember:

How you spend the minutes of each day add up to how you spend your life.

The End...

You've reached the end...**congrats**!

However, while you've reached the end of this book, you're only just beginning. Now, go out into your world and make it happen.

Find out what's important to you. Create the space you need to make things happen. And, finally, take action!

I've enjoyed sharing these ideas with you today. I hope you enjoyed reading them.

Have an outstanding life; full of joy, happiness, and success!

Weston Lyon

keep reading ⟶

I put some valuable resources in the back of this book for you; in case you need them☺

For Coaches

The best way I know of to leap frog over your competition and position yourself as one of the leading authorities in your field is to **Write a Book!**

Your own book will not only position you as an authority in your market, it will:

- **Add an additional money-making revenue stream** to your business...while you sleep!
- **Leverage your time**, so you can work with the best of the best, cream-of-the-crop clients YOU CHOOSE to work with.
- **Magnetically attract clients** who are dying to work with you and pay you what you deserve
- **And much more!**

ONE DOWNSIDE THOUGH: Writing a book can be a daunting task...actually, it can be downright *scary*.

But <u>have no fear</u>. There is a way to write and publish a book...and to do it FAST! For more details, go here, now...before your competition does:

www.CoachesBecomeAuthors.com

For Solo-Entrepreneurs

There are 2 secrets every entrepreneur must learn to master in order to be successful in business:

1. **You must master your marketing**. Marketing is the art of getting clients and customers to walk in your door, go to your website, or pick up the phone and call you. Without them, you're dead in the water. This skill is crucial!

2. **You must master your time**. Your time is your most valuable asset. Listen, if you cannot manage and master your time properly, you'll always be behind schedule; never getting enough done; stressing yourself out, day and night. It's essential to master this skill.

For more information on how to master both your marketing and your time, as well as to learn more secrets for succeeding as an entrepreneur, go here now:

www.SecretsForEntrepreneurs.com

Books by Weston Lyon

Secrets for Coaches: How to Write a Book Fast!
$14.95

Leadership Starts with YOU!
$14.95

These books and all other books by Weston Lyon can be found on **www.WestonLyon.com**.

For Special Quantity Orders, contact Weston Lyon at **866-709-1683** or at **westonlyon@westonlyon.com**.

****

Quotes by Weston Lyon

"Success is all your fault."

"Clarity is KING. When life gets complicated, slow down and focus on what you want."

"Success is learning from your mistakes and trying something new until it works."

"Shoot for excellence, not perfection."

"Extreme Clarity + Intense Focus + Pure Desire + Fast Action = Success in all areas of your life"

About Weston Lyon

Weston Lyon is the author of 14 books and a passionate professional speaker.

Weston's entrepreneurial path has been a long one for only being 30 years young. He started his first business at age 20; and has since been involved in multiple businesses, ranging from skin care, to janitorial services, to gift incentive sales, to fitness coaching, to marketing and publishing.

Today, Weston continues to have his hands in multiple businesses with the majority of his time spent writing and speaking to coaches and solo-entrepreneurs; as well as college students, when he gets the opportunity.

Weston lives in Sewickley; a small town outside Pittsburgh, PA. When he's not working, he's either on the playground with his son, Haven; or he's having fun practicing mixed marital arts, yoga, rock climbing, roller-blading, or any other adventurous, athletic activity he has the chance to do.

Speaking Engagements

Weston Lyon is available for speaking engagements at conferences, colleges, seminars, and schools. For more information on topics and availability go to:

www.WestonLyon.com

If the web isn't your thing, contact Weston Lyon at:
westonlyon@westonlyon.com
or
866-709-1683

****

Write to Weston Lyon

Weston loves hearing from fans and customers! Please feel free to contact Weston with your success stories, questions, or suggestions:
westonlyon@westonlyon.com
or
866-709-1683
or
Weston Lyon
6 McCabe St.
Sewickley, PA 15143

www.ingramcontent.com/pod-product-compliance
Lightning Source LLC
Chambersburg PA
CBHW051532170526
45165CB00002B/700